Flamingo

Patricia Whitehouse

Heinemann Library
Chicago, Illinois

© 2003 Reed Educational & Professional Publishing
Published by Heinemann Library,
an imprint of Reed Educational & Professional Publishing,
Chicago, Illinois

Customer Service 888-454-2279
Visit our website at www.heinemannlibrary.com

Designed by Sue Emerson, Heinemann Library
Printed and bound in the United States by Lake Book Manufacturing, Inc.

07 06 05 04 03
10 9 8 7 6 5 4 3 2 1

Library of Congress Cataloging-in-Publication Data
Whitehouse, Patricia, 1958-
    Flamingo / Patricia Whitehouse.
       p. cm. — (Zoo animals)
Includes index.
Summary: An introduction to flamingos, including their size, diet and everyday life style, which highlights differences between those in the wild and those living in a zoo habitat.
    ISBN: 1-58810-901-1 (HC), 1-40340-646-4 (Pbk.)
    1. Flamingos—Juvenile literature. [1. Flamingos. 2. Zoo animals.] I. Title.
    QL696.C56 W55 2002
    598.3'5—dc21

                            2001006873

Acknowledgments
The author and publishers are grateful to the following for permission to reproduce copyright material:
Title page, pp. 6, 22, 24 Rob & Ann Simpson/Visuals Unlimited; p. 4 Gerry Ellis/Minden Pictures; p. 5 Carl & Ann Parcell/Corbis; p. 7 M. C. Chamberlain/DRK Photo; p. 8 M. P. Kahl/Bruce Coleman Inc.; p. 9 Michael Wickes/Bruce Coleman Inc.; pp. 10, 12, 19 M. P. Kahl/DRK Photo; p. 11 Morton Beebe/Corbis; p. 13 David Bull/Audubon Zoo; p. 14 Tui de Roy/Minden Pictures; p. 15 Tim Fitzharris/Minden Pictures; p. 16 James P. Rowan/DRK Photo; p. 17 Larry Lipsky/DRK Photos; p. 18 Barbara C. Rowell/DRK Photos; p. 20 Gallo Images/Corbis; p. 21 Chicago Zoological Society/Brookfield Zoo; p. 23 (row 1, L-R) M. C. Chamberlain/DRK Photo, Russell Illig/PhotoDisc, Gerry Ellis/Minden Pictures; p. 23 (row 2, L-R) M. P. Kahl/Bruce Coleman Inc., David Bull/Audubon Zoo, Science Pictures Limited/Corbis; p. 23 (row 3, L-R) Chicago Zoological Society/The Brookfield Zoo, Morton Beebe/Corbis, Jim Schulz/Chicago Zoological Society/The Brookfield Zoo; back cover (L-R) M.C. Chamberlain/DRK Photo, Bruce Coleman Inc.

Cover photograph by Rob & Ann Simpson/Visuals Unlimited
Photo research by Bill Broyles

Every effort has been made to contact copyright holders of any material reproduced in this book. Any omissions will be rectified in subsequent printings if notice is given to the publisher.

Special thanks to our advisory panel for their help in the preparation of this book:

Eileen Day, Preschool Teacher
Chicago, IL

Ellen Dolmetsch,
Library Media Specialist
Wilmington, DE

Kathleen Gilbert,
Teacher
Round Rock, TX

Sandra Gilbert,
Library Media Specialist
Houston, TX

Angela Leeper,
Educational Consultant
North Carolina Department
of Public Instruction
Raleigh, NC

Pam McDonald, Reading Teacher
Winter Springs, FL

Melinda Murphy,
Library Media Specialist
Houston, TX

We would also like to thank Lee Haines, Assistant Director of Marketing and Public Relations at the Brookfield Zoo in Brookfield, Illinois, for his review of this book.

Some words are shown in bold, **like this.**
You can find them in the picture glossary on page 23.

Contents

What Are Flamingos?

Flamingos are birds.

Birds have **feathers** and lay eggs.

In the wild, flamingos live where it is warm all year.

But you can see flamingos at the zoo.

What Do Flamingos Look Like?

neck

feathers

Flamingos have pink **feathers**.

They have long necks and long legs.

Flamingos have curved, orange and black **bills.**

Their eyes are yellow-orange.

What Do Baby Flamingos Look Like?

Baby flamingos have white **feathers** and straight, red **bills**.

Baby flamingos are called **chicks**.

8

New chicks have short legs.

They look more like their parents
as they get older.

Where Do Flamingos Live?

In the wild, flamingos live by water.

Some live near the ocean.

In some zoos, flamingos live in outdoor **lagoons.**

Other zoos keep flamingos in **enclosures** with water and plants.

What Do Flamingos Eat?

In the wild, flamingos eat bugs and **shrimp.**

They take their food from the water with their **bills.**

At the zoo, flamingos eat a special soup.

It is made with ground-up **grain** and meat.

What Do Flamingos Do All Day?

Flamingos spend a lot of time eating.

They also take care of their **feathers**.

Flamingos rest standing in the water.

They also take baths in the water.

How Do Flamingos Sleep?

Flamingos sleep standing on one leg.

They fold their necks and heads onto their bodies.

leg joint

When flamingos sleep, their **leg joint** locks shut.

This keeps their leg straight, so they can stand for a long time.

What Sounds Do Flamingos Make?

Flamingos are very noisy birds.

They can honk like **geese**.

They can also grunt like a pig!

They do this to get other flamingos to pay attention.

How Are Flamingos Special?

Wild flamingos are pink because of the food they eat.

Without that food, they would be gray.

Zookeepers give zoo flamingos a special oil.

It makes their **feathers** bright pink.

Quiz

Do you remember what these flamingo parts are called?

Look for the answers on page 24.

?

?

?

Picture Glossary

bill
pages 7, 8, 12

goose
(more than one are geese)
page 18

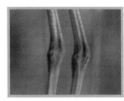

leg joint
page 17

chick
pages 8, 9

grain
page 13

shrimp
page 12

enclosure
page 11

lagoon
page 11

zookeeper
page 21

feathers
pages 4, 6, 8, 14, 21

23

Note to Parents and Teachers

Reading for information is an important part of a child's literacy development. Learning begins with a question about something. Help children think of themselves as investigators and researchers by encouraging their questions about the world around them. Each chapter in this book begins with a question. Read the question together. Look at the pictures. Talk about what you think the answer might be. Then read the text to find out if your predictions were correct. Think of other questions you could ask about the topic, and discuss where you might find the answers. Assist children in using the picture glossary and the index to practice new vocabulary and research skills.

Index

Answers to quiz on page 22

bill

feathers

leg joint